MW01600522

The Just Shall Live By Faith

God has not given us a spirit of fear; but of power, and of love, and of a sound mind (2 Timothy 1:7)

Printed in the United States of America:
First print 2018

Disclamier: This book is intended to provide inspirational and
educational content. The author and publisher are not responsible
for any actions taken by readers based on the information provided
herein. Readers are encouraged to consult appropriate professionals
for specific advice tailored to their situation.

Prayer

Heavenly Father,

I come before You with a heart seeking to understand and embody the truth that " the just shall live by faith". Your word teaches that righteousness comes through faith in Jesus Christ, not by our own deeds. Father, I acknowledge that faith is the assurance of things hoped for, the conviction of things not seen. It's through faith that we please You, trusting in Your promises even when circumstances challenge us.

Strengthen our faith, O God. Help us to trust in Your word, to rely on Your guidance, and to walk in obedience. When doubts arise, remind us of Your faithfulness. When fear threatens, fill us with courage rooted in trust. May our life reflect a steadfast faith, demonstrating love, patience, and hope. Let our actions be a testament to the transformative power of living by faith.
Thank You for the gift of faith and the righteousness that comes through it. Guide us daily to live in a manner worthy of this calling.

In Jesus' name, I pray.
Amen.

Letter From Sheunda

It gives me great joy to write this book... The Just Shall Live By Faith. Your decision in purchasing this book is wonderful and it warms my heart knowing that you're interested in getting an understanding of what faith is. God has given us a lot of tools to use in order to fulfill our destiny in life. and operating in Faith is one of the greatest gifts that was given to us. Let me inform you, that without faith it's impossible to please God. If you're tired of just surviving and ready to start *living by faith*, this is your moment. In this powerful book, I will walk you through the foundation, function, and fire of what it truly means to live by faith. Rooted in scripture, and alive with personal insight,The Just Shall Live By Faith isn't just a book, it's a call to action. With reflection questions, prayers, declarations, and more, this book will challenge, equip, and inspire you to live the life God has called you to. So before you step into the book... clear your mind, have a bible, and a pen to answer all questions that are being asked.

Remember: You are the just. AND the just shall live; FULLY, FREELY, and FEARLESSLY by faith.

Your Author,
Sheunda

Table of Contents

- Faith Declarations
- Faith Journal Prompts
- Final Encouragement

Introduction: Embracing a Life of Faith

FAITH is more than a belief system. It's a lifestyle- a daily decision to trust God even when everything around you says not to. It's waking up with Questions but choosing to move forward anyway, believing that God is who He says He is and that His promises are still true." The just shall by faith ". This powerful declaration is found throughout Scripture- from Habakkuk (2:4)to Romans (1:17) to Galatians (3:11) and Hebrew (10:38). It's not a suggestion. It's a standard. It's the way of life for those who have been made right with God- not through works, but believing in the finished work of Jesus Christ. But what does it really means to live by faith? Who are the "just"? How is faith developed, and what happens when it's put to the test? In this book, we'll explore those questions and more. We'll uncovered what faith truly is, and what it's not. We'll talk about why faith is essential for every believer, how it grows, how it manifests, and what its looks like when it becomes more than just words, it becomes your walk.

This is not just theology. It's personal. I've wrestled with doubt, fear, and uncertainly. I've stood at the edge of decision, where faith was the only thing I could hold on to. I know what it means to live by faith because I've had to - and I want to help you do the same.

Whether you're new to your walk with God or you've been in this journey for years, The Just Shall Live By Faith is for you. It's a call to live boldly, stand firmly, and walk daily in the truth that faith is not optional- it's the foundation.

Let's take this journey together

Section 1: Who Are "The Just" Key points:

- Definition of "The Just" : In Christian theology, " the just" refers to those who have been justified by faith in Jesus Christ, not by their own works (Romans 3:28).
- Justification Explained: Justification is a legal term signifying God's declaration of a sinner being righteous through faith in Christ. It's a one-time act that changes our standing before God.
- Old Testament Examples: Abraham believed God, and it was credited to him as righteousness (Genesis 15:6). Similarly, David spoke of the blessedness of the one to whom God credits righteousness apart from works (Romans 4:6).

Section 1: Who are the Just?

When the Bible declares, "The just shall live by faith," it doesn't leave us guessing about who the just one are. The just are those who have been made right with God- not through perfection, not through performance, but through faith in Jesus Christ. Many people think of the word " just" and immediately associate it with being morally upright or flawless. But that's not how God defines it. The word " just " in Scripture refers to those who have been justified- declare righteous- not because of what they've done, but because of what Jesus did on the cross. Romans 5:1 tells us, "Therefore, since we have been justified by faith, we have peace with God through our Lord Jesus Christ. " That's where it starts. To be just is to be in right standing with God. It means that when God looks at you, He sees you through the lens of Jesus' sacrifice, not your flaws or failures. But let me be clear: being "just' is not about having it all together. It's about surrender. It's about believing God enough to trust His way not your own. The just are the ones who say, " I may not be perfect , but I know who is- and I'm trusting Him with my life".

Justified by faith, Not works: One of the greatest lies the enemy tries to sell us is that we have to earn our place with God. That if we pray enough, give enough, behave well enough- we'll finally be acceptable to Him. But Ephesians 2:8-9 shuts that down completely: " For it is by grace you have been saved, through faith- and this is not from yourselves, it is the gift of God- not by works, so that no one can boast". The just don't live on a spiritual treadmill trying to impress God. The just live from a place of rest, knowing that the price has already been paid.

A New Identity:

Being justified changes your identity. It shifts how you see yourself. You're no longer just your past, your mistakes, or your weakness. You're a new creation (2 Corinthians 5:17). You're someone God has called righteous- not because you never did wrong, but because you now live by faith in the One who made you right. When you truly understand that you are justified, you will stop chasing validation from people, platforms, or position. You will stop performing for acceptance and start walking in the confidence of who God says you are.

The Just Live Differently: Being justified changes, means you've been marked. You don't respond to life like the world does. You're not driven by fear, greed, or self. You're guided by faith.

You take steps not because you see the full picture, but because you trust the One who does. You forgive when it's hard. You love when it's inconvenient. You keep going when others quit, not because you have it all together, but because you know who holds you together.

You Are the Just:

If you've put faith in Jesus Christ, you are the just. That's your position. That's your foundation. And this book is your invitation to not just know it, but live it, So many of us walk around with spiritual amnesia, forgetting who we are and who we belong to. But it's time to wake up. It's time to rise and walk in the truth that you are justified, and you are called to live, not by fear, not by doubt, not by flesh, but by faith.

Reflection Questions: Section 1

1. Have I truly received God's gift of justification through faith?

_____

_____

_____

_____

_____

2. In what ways have I tried to earn God's acceptance?

_____

_____

_____

_____

_____

3. How does knowing I'm justified by faith impact the way I see myself?

_____

_____

_____

_____

_____

4. What would change in my life if I truly believed I was already made right with God?

_____

_____

_____

_____

_____

5. What does it mean to be "just" or "righteous" in the context of Scripture?

_____

_____

_____

_____

6. How is justification achieved according to Roman's 3:28?

_____

_____

_____

_____

7. In what ways did Abraham exemplify being "just" through faith?

_____

_____

_____

_____

8. How does understanding my identity as " the just" influence my daily live?

_____

_____

_____

_____

Section 2: What Faith is and isn't Key Points:

- Biblical Definition: Hebrews 11:1 describes faith as " the assurance of things hoped for, the conviction of things not seen". Faith involves trust in God's promises, even when they are not yet visible.
- Faith vs. Presumption: Faith is not presuming upon God to act according to our desire but trusting Him to act according to His will. It's not a tool to manipulate outcomes but a relationship of trust.
- Faith vs. Works: While faith leads to good works, it is not synonymous with them. Works are the fruit of genuine faith, not the root of our justification.

Section 2: What Faith is and isn't:

Ask ten different people what faith is, and you might hear ten different answers. For some, faith is just a feeling. For others, it's a religious label. Some think it's blind hope, like tossing a prayer into the sky and hoping for the best. But if we're going to live by faith, we need to know what it really is and what it's not.

Faith is Confidence in God's Character:

Hebrews 11:1 says, " Now faith is the substance of things hoped for, the evidence of things not seen". That verse doesn't say faith is a wish. It says it's substance and evidence. Faith is real. It's not abstract. It's not vague. It's not weak. Faith is spiritual substance. It's trusting in the unseen because you know the One who sees all. Faith isn't just believing God can do something. It's believing that He will, not always in the way we want, but always in the way that's best.

Faith says," Even if I don't understand, I trust You."
Faith says, "Even if the door closes, I still believe You're good."
Faith says, " I may not see it yet, but I believe it's already done."

Faith Is Not a Shortcut to Control:

Let's be honest. Sometimes we want faith to be a formula. We want to check the right boxes, say the right words, and get the outcome we desire. But true faith doesn't control God, it surrenders to Him.

Faith is Anchored in God's Word:

Romans 10:17 " Faith comes by hearing, and hearing by the word of God." Your faith will only be as strong as what you feed it. If you're constantly listening to fear, doubt, and negativity, faith will weaken. But if you're rooted in the Word, your faith will grow strong and unshakable.This is why the enemy fights to distract you from reading the Bible, because he knows the Word builds your faith, and faith makes you dangerous. Faith is a Lifestyle, Not a Moment: Faith isn't something you turn on when you're in trouble. It's how you live every day. The just live by faith, not just believe in it once. This means trusting God with your relationships, your career, your healing, your calling, your family, your everything. And when you walk by faith, you start to see life differently. You don't panic when the world shakes. You don't fold under pressure. You stand, because you know who holds you up.

Define faith from a biblical perspective. Hebrews 11:1 describes faith as " the assurance of things hoped for, the conviction of things not seen." Clarify that faith is not mere wishful thinking or blind optimism. Instead, it's a confident trust in God's promises and character. Contrast true faith with misconception, such as equating faith with positive affirmations or self- generated belief systems.

Reflection Questions: Section 2

1.How does Hebrews 11:1 define faith, and what implications does this have for believers?

_____

_____

_____

_____

2. What are common misconceptions about faith, and how can they be addressed?

_____

_____

_____

_____

3. How does faith differ from mere optimism or positive thinking?

_____

_____

_____

_____

4. Why is it important to distinguish between genuine faith and presumption?

_____

_____

_____

_____

Reflection Questions: Section 2

5. What definition of faith have you believed in the past? Do it align with God's word?

_____

_____

_____

_____

 6. Have you been trying to use faith to control outcomes instead of trusting God's plan?

_____

_____

_____

_____

7. In what areas of your life are you struggling to walk by faith?

_____

_____

_____

_____

8. How can you build Your faith through God's Word this week?

_____

_____

_____

_____

Section 3: Why Faith Is Essential: Key Points

- Pleasing God: Without faith, it's impossible to please God Hebrews 11:6. Faith is the means by which we approach and relate to Him.
- Salvation: We are saved by grace through faith, not by works (Ephesians 2:8-9). Faith is the channel through which we receive God's gift of salvation.
- Living the Believer life : Means by which we live daily. The righteous live by faith, trusting God in every circumstance.

Sections 3: Why Faith Is Essential

You can't walk with God without faith. You can go to Chruch every Sunday, know all the worship songs, and even quote a few scriptures. But without faith, you'll never step into the life God truly has for you. Why? Because faith is the key that unlocks your relationship with Him. Hebrews 11:6 says, "And without it is impossible to please God, because anyone who comes to Him must believe that He exists and that He rewards those who earnestly seek Him". It doesn't say it's hard to please God without faith, it says it's impossible.

Faith is How We're Saved:

Salvation doesn't come by works, good behavior, or spiritual effort. It comes through one door: faith in Jesus Christ. Ephesians 2:8-9 puts it plainly: "For it is by grace you have been saved, through faith, and this is not from yourselves, it is the gift of God, not by works, so that no one can boast."

Grace is the gift.
Faith is the access.
Jesus is the reason.
If you don't have faith, you can't receive the gift. It's like having a wrapped present in your hands but refusing to open it.

Faith Is How We Live:
Faith isn't just the starting point of the Believers life, it's the whole path.

Romans 1:17 says, " The just shall live by faith." That means our decisions, our direction, our attitude, and our trust are rooted in faith.

Faith teaches us to:
- Obey when we don't understand.
- Trust when we can't see.
- Stand when we feel like falling.
- Keep going when life says stop.

Without faith, we're guided by fear, feelings, and the opinions of people. With faith, we're anchored in God's truth, even when the storm is raging.

Faith Is How We Overcome:

Life brings battles. And you don't win spiritual battles with natural weapons. You win them by faith.
1 John 5:4 says, " This is the victory that has overcome the world, even our faith." Your faith is a weapon. It's not passive. It's not quiet. It's powerful. It silences lies, resist the enemy, and declares, I will not be moved. That's why the enemy targets your faith. He knows if he can get you to stop believing , he can get you to stop moving. But when your faith is alive, your purpose stays active, and your impact becomes unstoppable.

Faith Is How We Receive from God:

Every promise in Scripture is activated by faith. Healing, provision, peace, breakthrough all of it flows through belief.
Mark 11:24 says, " Whatever you ask for in prayer, believe that you have received it, and it will be yours." God doesn't responds to believing. Faith doesn't make God move, faith positions you to receive what He's already done.

Faith Is How We Please God

There are many things we can do for God, but what touches His heart the most is faith. He's not impressed by our perfection, He's drawn to our trust. Throughout the Bible, you'll notice a pattern: whenever Jesus performed a miracle, He often responded with these words. " Your faith has made you whole." Not your status. Not your background . Not your religious knowledge. Your faith.God is still looking for that kind of faith today.

Faith is Essential Because God is Invisible

Let's be real, you've never seen God with your physical eyes. You've never heard Him with your natural ears. And yet, you believe. That's faith. We live by faith because we follow a God we can't see, trusting that He's working even when we don't feel Him. And as we grow, faith becomes our spiritual eyesight, helping us walk confidently even when the path ahead is unclear.

So Why Is Faith Essential? Because it's the only way to:

- Know God
- Please God
- Receive from God
- Overcome the world
- Walk In Your purpose
- Live a life that lasts

You can't live without it, not spiritually. That's why they just don't visit faith occasionally, we live by it.

Explore the necessity of faith in the Believers life. Faith is the means by which we are justified before God (Galatians 3:11). It's through faith that we receive salvation, experience God's grace, and live in obedience. Without faith, it's impossible to please God (Hebrews 11:6). Faith empowers believers to endure trials, make godly decisions, and live victoriously.

Reflection Questions :Section 3

1. According to Hebrew 11:6, why is faith indispensable in our relationship with God?

_____

_____

_____

_____

2. How does faith serve as the foundation for our salvation and daily walk with Christ?

_____

_____

_____

_____

3.In What ways does faith empower us to overcome life's challenges?

_____

_____

_____

_____

4. How does living by faith affect our interactions with others and our community?

_____

_____

_____

_____

Reflection Questions: Section 3

5.Have I treated faith as a one-time decision or a daily lifestyle?

_____

_____

_____

_____

6. In What areas of my life am I depending on feelings more than faith?

_____

_____

_____

_____

7. What's one situation right now where I need. Activate my faith?

_____

_____

_____

_____

8. What promise from God am I struggling to believe? Why?

_____

_____

_____

_____

Section 4 : How Faith Is Developed

Key Points:

- Hearing the Word: Faith comes by hearing, and hearing through the word of Christ (Romans 10:17). Regular engagement with Scripture strengthens faith.
- Obedience: Putting God's Word into practice reinforces our trust in Him. As we obey, we experience His faithfulness, which in turn deepens our faith.
- Community: Surrounding ourselves with fellow believers encourages and builds our faith. Shared testimonies and mutual support are vital.

Section 4: How Faith Is Developed

You weren't meant to just have faith, you were meant to grow in it. Faith is like a seed planted in the soil of your spirit. But just like a seed, if it's not watered, nourished, and exposed to the right conditions, it won't grow. The good news is: God has already given you the measure of faith (Romans 12:3). The challenge is learning how to develop it so you can walk in the full power and purpose He's designed for your life.

Faith Comes by Hearing: Romans 10;17 says, " So then faith comes by hearing, and hearing by the word of God." You can't grow in faith if you're not feeding your spirit. Faith doesn't grow by chance, it grows by intentional exposure to the Word. Every time you open your Bible, listen to a message, or meditate on God's promises, you're planting and watering the seeds of faith. The more you hear God's voice, the less you'll be shaken by the noise of the world. This is why spiritual warfare often begins with distraction. If the enemy can keep you from the Word, he can keep you from faith. But when you stay in the Word, your faith begins to take root.

Faith Is Strengthened Through Testing. It doesn't sounds pretty, but it's true, faith grows best in the fire. James 1:3 says, ' The testing produces perseverance.' We don't like to be tested. We don't like uncertainty. But testing reveals what kind of faith we really have.

Think about it, you don't know how strong a bridge is until something heavy drives across it. In the same way, we don't know the strength of our faith until pressure, delay, or difficulty steps in. The storm doesn't come to destroy you, it comes to develop you. The trial isn't proof that God is gone, it's proof that your faith is about to be upgraded.

Faith Grows Through Obedience: You can hear the Word all day, but if you don't act on it, faith remains stagnant. James 2:17 says, " Faith by itself, if it is not accompanied by action, is dead." Every step of obedience is like lifting a spiritual weight. The more you walk in obedience especially when it's uncomfortable. The more faith is stretched and strengthened.

Obedience is faith in motion.
When God says "go" and you move ... that's faith.
When God says " wait," and you stay...that's faith too.
Real faith shows up in your decisions. Not just in what you say, but in what you do.

Faith Is Built in Community: You weren't designed to grow in faith alone. Hebrew 10:24-25 encourages us to stir one another up and not neglect meeting together. Why? Because faith is contagious. Hearing someone else's testimony can water the seeds of your own. Praying with others can reignite your

Connfidence in God's power. Being challenge by someone further along in faith can call you higher. Isolation weakens faith, but connection strengthens it.

Faith Is Fueled by Remembering: One of the quickest ways to lose faith is to forget what God has already done. When the Israelites faced new battles, God constantly reminded them, " I am the Lord who brought you out of Egypt. " In other words, "Don't forget what I've already done for you". Psalm 77:11 says, " I will remember the deeds Of the Lord; yes, I will remember your miracles of long ago". Sometimes the key to developing faith is rehearsing old victories. Keep a faith journal. Write down what God has done in the past. Go back and re-read it when you're in a dry season. Let your past deliverances become fuel for your future belief.

Faith Develops Over Time: Let's be real, faith development isn't always fast. Sometimes you'll feel strong and bold. Other times you'll feel like you're barely holding on. And that's okay. Growth takes time. What matters is that you keep showing up. You keep praying, keep believing , keep trusting, even if it's only mustard seed sized. Jesus said, " If you have faith as small as a mustard seed… nothing will be impossible for you." (Matthew 17:20). It's not about the size, it's about the direction.

So, How is Faith Developed?
- By hearing the Word of God consistently
- Through tests and trials that stretch you
- By acting in obedience, not just believing in theory
- By walking in community, not isolation
- Through remembering God's past faithfulness
- By being patient with the process

Faith development isn't always not about striving, it's about surrender. It's not about being impressive, it's about being consintent. As you commit to the process, you'll look back and realize; you didn't just grow in faith, faith carried you.

Faith comes by hearing the Word of God (Romans 10:17). Engaging in spiritual disciplines, such as prayer, Bible study, worship, and fellowship, strengthens our faith. Highlight the role of the Holy Spirit in nurturing faith and the importance of perseverance through life's challenges.

Reflection Questions: Section 4

1. What role does hearing and studying God's Word play in
   developing faith (Romans 10:17)

_____

_____

_____

_____

2. How do trials and challenges contribute to the strengthening of
your faith?

_____

_____

_____

_____

3. What spiritual disciplines are essential for nurturing and
growing your faith?

_____

_____

_____

_____

4. How does fellowship with other believers influence your faith
journey?

_____

_____

_____

_____

Reflection Questions: Section 4

5. Am I consistently feeding my faith through God's Word?

_____

_____

_____

_____

6. How have past test grown my faith, even if I didn't realize it at the time?

_____

_____

_____

_____

7. Is there something God is asking me to obey, even if it doesn't make sense?

_____

_____

_____

_____

8. Who am I surrounding myself with that helps build my faith?

_____

_____

_____

_____

Section 5: What Happens When Faith Is Manifested

Key Points:
- Doctrine: Faith shapes our beliefs, aligning them with biblical truth.
- Worship: A life of faith is marked by genuine worship, both individually and corporately.
- Morality: Faith influences our actions, leading to a life that reflects God's character.

Section 5: What Happens When Faith Is Manifested

Faith doesn't just sit still. Real faith moves, acts, and manifests. When faith goes from internal belief to external demonstration, things start to shift. Atmospheres change. Chains break. Miracles happen. And most importantly, God gets the glory.The Bible is filled with people whose faith wasn't just private belief, it was a public force. Faith that's manifested becomes a testimony. It speaks louder than your fears, louder than your past, and louder than the voices that said you couldn't.

Manifested Faith Produces Action: Faith without action is just theory. But manifested faith leads to movement. Think of the women with the issue of blood (Mark5:25-34). She didn't just believe Jesus could heal her, she acted on that belief. She pressed through the crowd, stretched her hand, and touched His garment. That was faith in motion. Jesus didn't say, " My power made you well." He said, " Your faith has made you whole." Faith that's alive moves toward what God has promised, even when fear is present.

Manifested Faith looks like:
  - Starting the business even when the funds aren't all there.
  - Forgiving even when your heart still feels broken.
  - Walking away from what's familiar because God said "go".
When faith shows up on the outside, heaven backs you up.

Manifested Faith Releases Power: Faith is the vehicle that carries God's power from the spiritual realm into the natural. Mark 2:5 tells the story of four friends who lowered a paralyzed man through a roof just to get him to Jesus. The Bible says, " When Jesus saw their faith…" not heard it, but He saw it, He healed the man and forgave his sins. That's the power of manifested faith. It doesn't wait for a perfect moment. It pushes through obstacles. It breaks tradition. It tears off roofs. When faith is seen, God responds. Not because He's impressed, but because that kind of faith aligns perfectly with His will.

Manifested Faith Inspires Others: When your faith comes alive, it doesn't just bless you, it blesses others too. Your breakthrough becomes someone else's encouragement. Your healing becomes someone else's hope. Your obedience becomes someone reminder that God is still moving.

Manifested faith is contagious:
People may argue theology, but they can't argue transformation. When others see what God has done in your life, it draws their hearts closer to Him. Let your life be living sermon. Let your story preach louder than your words. Because when faith is real, its shows.

Manifested Faith Attracts Resistance: Let's be real: when your faith starts manifesting, so will your enemies. Don't be surprised when the enemy turns up the heat the moment you start walking boldly. Faith puts you on the radar of both heaven and hell. But don't let that scare you, let it prepare you. Opposition is proof that you're making spiritual progress. The good news? The same faith that manifests blessing is the same faith that will carry you through battles. When faith shows up, God fights for you.

Manifested Faith Brings Glory to God: Ultimately, every act of faith points back to God's goodness. Matthew 5: 16 says, " Let your light shine before others, that they may see your good deeds and glorify your Father in heaven." When your life reflects faith, it becomes a billboard for God's grace. **Every yes. Every step. Every leap.** It all points back to the One who made it possible. Faith manifested is God's invitation to show off through your life, not for your fame, but for His glory.

So What Happens When Faith is Manifested?
- You move from hope to action
- God's power is released into your situation
- Others are inspired to believe
- Resistance may rise, but so will you
- God gets the glory, and your life becomes a testimony

Examine how genuine faith manifests in a believer's life. Faith influences our actions, decisions, and interactions with others. It produces fruit such as love, kindness, patience, and self-control (Galatians 5:22-23). Discuss how faith leads to good works, not as a means of earning salvation, but as evidence of a transformed life. Emphasize that faith impacts every area of life, including relationships, work, and community involvement.

Reflection Questions: Section 5

1. What are the visible signs of a life lived by faith?

_____

_____

_____

_____

2. How does faith influence your decisions, action, and reactions in daily life?

_____

_____

_____

_____

3. In what ways does genuine faith produce spiritual fruit (Galatians 5:22-23)

_____

_____

_____

_____

4. How can our faith positively impact those around us and our broader community?

_____

_____

_____

_____

Reflection Questions: Section 5

5. What has God called you to act on that you only been thinking about?

_____

_____

_____

_____

6. Has your faith been private or public? What would it look like for it to be seen?

_____

_____

_____

_____

7. Who in my life could be inspired by my testimony of faith?

_____

_____

_____

_____

_____

8. What opposition have I faced while walking in faith, and how did God show up?

_____

_____

_____

_____

Section 6: The Bottom Line: Living by Faith

Key Points:

- Continuous Journey: Living by faith is an ongoing process, requiring daily trust in God

- Challenges and Triumphs: Faith enables us to navigate life's difficulties and celebrate its joys with a God-centered perspective.

- Eternal Perspective: Faith keeps our focus on eternal realities, motivating us to live with purpose and hope.

Section 6: The Bottom Line…Living by Faith

So what's the bottom line? Faith isn't just a moment. It's a lifestyle. It's not a switch you flip on when life gets hard or when you need a miracle. Faith is how you breathe, walk, move, and make decisions every single day. It's how you love, how you endure, how you dream, and how you keep going when everything around you says stop. Faith isn't just for the spiritual elite or the deeply religious. Faith is for the just. That's YOU. That's ME. And it's not optional, it's essential.

Living by Faith Is Daily: Faith must become your default, not your last resort. You live by faith when:
- You choose peace in the middle of chaos.
- You give when you barely have enough.
- You obey God's leading when the path ahead isn't clear.
- You speak life over yourself when your emotions scream the opposite.

Living by faith isn't always flashy. It often looks quiet,insistent,and obedient. But don't mistake simple for powerless, God moves through steady faith just as much as He does through mountain, moving miracles.

Living by Faith Means You Trust the Process: Let's be honest, faith won't always give you fast results. Sometimes, living by faith means waiting on God when your flesh wants to fix it yourself .

It means trusting Him through delay, disappointment, and detours, knowing He's still working behind the scenes. Faith doesn't promise an easy road. It promises a victorious outcome. And here's the truth: you may not always feel strong, but if you can keep believing , even when you're tired…you're living by faith.

Living by Faith Makes You Unshakable: Storms may come. The economy may shift. People may walk away. But when you live by faith, you won't fall apart, because your foundation is secure. Psalm 125:1 says, "Those who trust in the lord are like Mount Zion, which cannot be shaken but endures forever."

Faith keeps you grounded when life gets loud.
It keeps you standing when you feel weak.
It keeps you pressing when giving up looks easier.
Living by faith isn't denying reality, its declaring that God's Word is a higher reality.

Living by Faith Puts God First: When you live by faith, God becomes your source, not just on Sunday, but all week long. You don't look to people, money, or status to define your worth or direction. You trust the One who wrote your story before you were ever born. Living by faith says, "God, I trust the facts. I trust You more than I trust my feelings. And I trust You more than I trust myself."

Living by Faith Is a Legacy: The greatest thing you can leave behind isn't a title, a house, or a business. It's a testimony of faith. When people remember your life, let them say, " She or He believed God. You walked by faith. You trusted God no matter what." Your faith may start with you, but it's designed to outlive you. It teaches your children, strengthens your friends, and inspires others long after you're gone.

The Bottom Line Is This:
- Faith is how we're made right with God.
- Faith is how we live out our purpose.
- Faith is how we endure the trails.
- Faith is how we experience the impossible.
- Faith is how we walk, not by sight, but by trust in the one who is faithful.

You are the just.And the just shall live, not survive, not exist, but truly live by faith. Summarize the key insights from the previous chapters. Reiterate that living by faith is not a one-time event but a continuous journey. Trust God daily, rely on His promises, and walk in obedience. Highlight the rewards of a faith-filled life, including peace, purpose, and eternal hope. Examine your own faith and take steps to deepen it.

Reflection Questions: Section:6

1.What does it means to live by faith on a daily basis?

_____

_____

_____

_____

2. How can I maintain faith during seasons of doubt or difficulty?

_____

_____

_____

_____

3.What are practical steps to ensure my life are consistently aligned with faith in God

_____

_____

_____

_____

4. How does living by faith prepare me for eternal life with God?

_____

_____

_____

_____

Reflection Questions: Section:6

5. Have I been living by faith daily or just in emergencies?

_____

_____

_____

_____

6. What area of my life is God calling me to trust Him more deeply?

_____

_____

_____

_____

7. How has my lifestyle changed as I've grown in faith?

_____

_____

_____

_____

8. What kind of faith legacy do I want to leave behind?

_____

_____

_____

_____

Conclusion: A Call to Live Boldly by Faith

You've made it to the end of this journey, but the real journey is just beginning. Faith is not something we master overnight. It's a daily walk. A moment-by-moment decision. A life long commitment to trust a faithful God, even when we can't trace His hand.

You now know who the just one.
You understand what faith is and what it isn't.
You've seen why it's essential, how it develops, and what it looks like when it manifests. And most of all, you've been called to live it.

The world doesn't need more perfect people. It needs more people of faith, people who believe when it's hard, obey when it's costly, and love when it's not convenient. Faith isn't about having all the answers. It about knowing Who the answer is. So take the pressure off. Let go of needing control. And step fully into the grace that allows you to live by faith, not by fear.

You are the just.
And your time to live by faith is now.

Go forward boldly. Trust deeply. Stan firmly.
And live a life that reflects the one who made you righteous.

Closing Prayer:

Father God,

Thank you for this journey. Thank you for the truth that the just shall live by faith. Thank you that You don't call me to walk by sight, but by trust in Your character, Your Word, and Your promises.

Lord, I surrender my doubts, my fears, and my need to have it all figured out. I choose to walk by faith. Strengthen me when I'm weary. Remind me of Your goodness when I'm unsure. Help me to trust You in the quiet seasons, the stormy ones, and that mountaintop moments. Let my life be a testimony of faith in action. Let my words, my choices, and my obedience point back to You. Teach me to live, to move, and to have my being fully rooted in You. I declare that I am the just. And by Your Spirit, I will live, not by what I see, not by what I feel, but by faith.

In Jesus name,
Amen

Faith Declarations

Bonus Section

I declare:

- I am justified by faith, not by works. (Romans 5:1)
- I walk by faith and not by sight. (2 Corinthians 5:7)
- My faith is growing stronger every day. (Romans 10:17)
- I trust God's timing, God's plan, and God's heart.
- I am unshakable because my foundation is Christ.
- When I can't see the way, I still believe God is making a way.
- I am not ruled by fear, doubt, or feeling, I am led by faith.
- I live, move, and speak from a place of divine confidence.
- My life is a testimony of the faithfulness of God.
- The just shall live by faith and I am the just!

Faith Journal Prompts:
Pause and Reflect with These Journal Questions:

1.What does "living by faith" looks like in my current season

_____

_____

_____

_____

_____

_____

2. What fears or mindsets do i need to surrender to walk in faith
more fully?

_____

_____

_____

_____

_____

3.When have I seen God come through for me in a powerful way?

_____

_____

_____

_____

_____

Faith Journal Prompts:
Pause and Reflect with These Journal Questions:

4. What are some scriptures I can meditate on when my faith feels weak?

_____
_____
_____
_____
_____

5. Where is God asking me to take a bold step of faith right now?

_____
_____
_____
_____
_____

REVISIT THESE QUESTION OFTEN✽

Final Encouragement

If you've made it this far, I want you to know; you are not reading this by accident. God is calling you to a deeper, stronger walk of faith. This isn't the end of the book, it's the beginning of your next bold chapter. Keep going . Keep trusting. Keep living by faith 💕

Author Bio

Sheunda White is an inspirational speaker, author, and devoted follower of Christ whose passion is to empower others to walk boldly in their God, given purpose. Known for her transparent storytelling and spiritual insight, fear, doubt, and life's toughest challenges through unwavering faith in God. With a heart for the lost and a mission to help people understand the power of the Holy Spirit, she equips readers with biblical truths that transform lives. Her ministry and message inspire people to believe they can do all things through Christ Jesus and to live with unshakable faith, no matter the circumstances.

Thank You

Thank you for your support and for joining me on this journey through faith. My prayer is that these pages have stirred something deep within you, a renewed passion to trust God with your whole heart and live bobly as one of the just.

Let's keep this faith journey together. You can connect with me for more encouragement, teaching, and inspiration:

 TicTok:@divine_talk_studio (Real Talk With MeMa)

Made in the USA
Columbia, SC
26 August 2025

61633510R00033